Daddy Daughter Day

Written by T. L. Wynne
Illustrated by Lisa Reid-Williamson

No part of this publication may be reproduced in whole or in part, or stored in a retrieval system, transmitted in any form or by any means, electronic, mechanical, photocopying, recording, or otherwise, without written permission of the publisher. For more information regarding permission, contact **i am me, LLC**. www.iammeinitiative.com

ISBN-978-0-9987915-7-9   Printed in USA

The Daddy Daughter series is based on the positive relationship between a father and his young daughter. Exuding the importance of a father's influence in his daughter's life, illustrating their relationship and exciting adventures together.

*Every moment we share
feels like a lifetime of happiness.*

-Dad

"Buckle up Princess it's time to go."

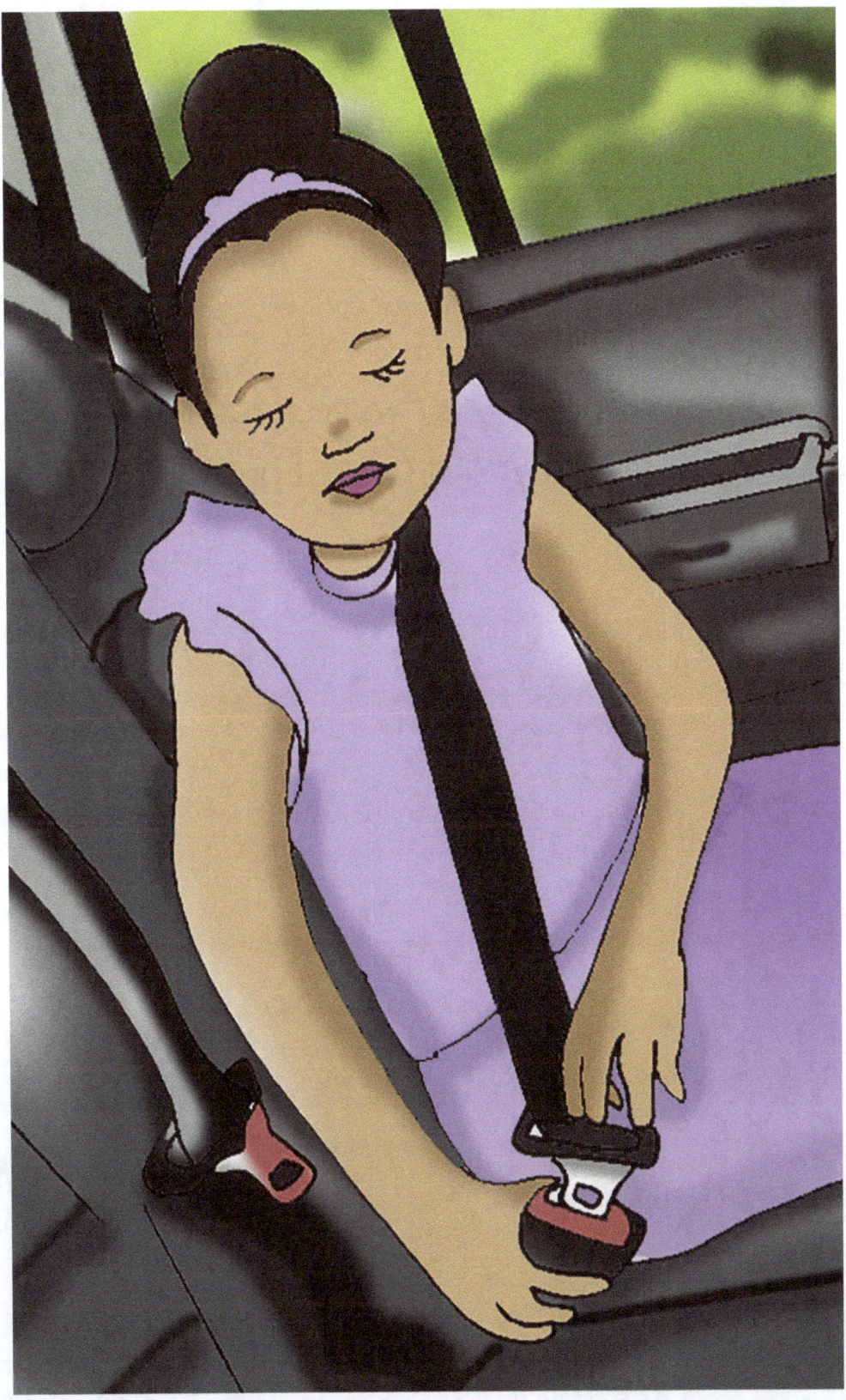

Where they were headed, Amiyah did not know.

As long as she was with Daddy, she knew it would be fun. Daddy always knew how to make her smile as bright as the sun.

They started off with breakfast at her favorite place.
Where she had her favorite pancakes, made like a silly face.

Next was the park where Amiyah loved to go down the slide.

They laughed and played,
and Daddy gave piggyback rides!

"The last stop is the mall, my little princess."

They went to her favorite store and she bought a beautiful new dress!

"But what's a new dress without pretty shoes?"

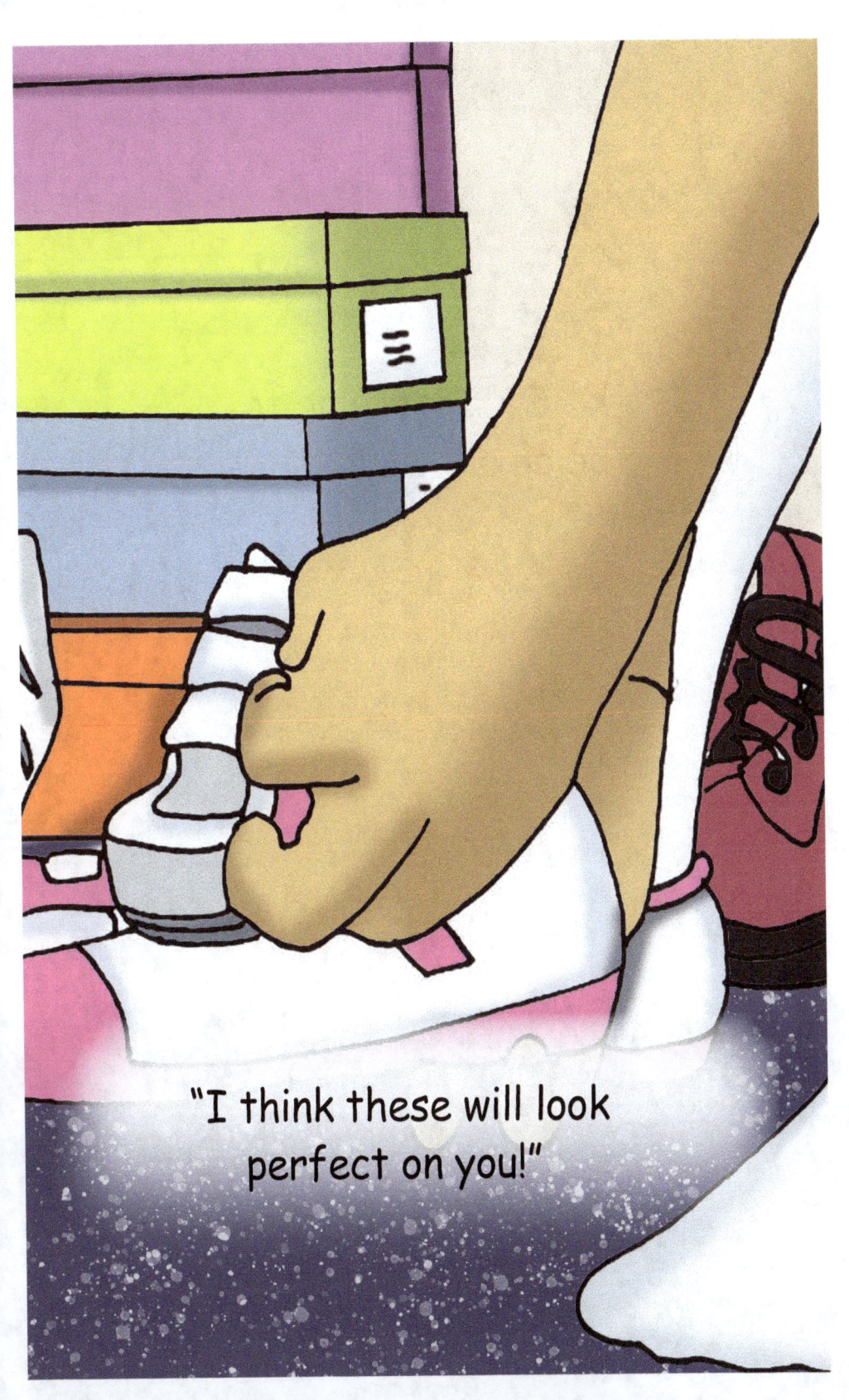

"Ok... Ok ... it's time to be on our way."